The Basic Essentials of
MINIMIZING IMPACT
ON THE WILDERNESS

by Michael Hodgson

**Illustrations by
Eric Gossler**

ICS BOOKS, Inc.
Merrillville, Indiana

THE BASIC ESSENTIALS OF MINIMIZING IMPACT ON THE WILDERNESS

Copyright © 1991 Michael Hodgson

10 9 8 7 6 5 4 3 2 1

Printed in U.S.A.

DEDICATION
Although many people have had a hand in shaping my sense of wilderness and environmental ethic, it is to parents, who instilled in me that sense of wonder and respect for all things, that I owe the greatest thanks. This book is for them.

ACKNOWLEDGMENTS
I wish to acknowledge The Boy Scouts of America, Crystal Lake Camps, Reini and Dotty Ross, and Adventure 16 for providng me with the background and knowledge necessary to write this book.

Published by:
ICS Books, Inc.
One Tower Plaza
107 E. 89th Avenue
Merrillville, IN 46410
800-541-7323

Library of Congress Cataloging-in-Publication Data

Hodgson, Michael.
    The basic essentials of minimizing impact on the wilderness / by Michael Hodgson.
        p.   cm. -- (The Essentials series)
        Includes index.
        ISBN 0-934802-78-5
        1. Outdoor recreation--Environmental aspects. 2. Wilderness areas--Recreational use.   I. Title.   II. Series.
    GV1991.6.H63 1991
    333.78'4--dc20   91-22569
                                                            CIP

TABLE OF CONTENTS

1. UNIVERSAL CONSIDERATIONS

Water Pollution
Soap
There is no such thing as biodegradable soap. Any soap will alter the pH value of the water if dumped directly into it and can adversely affect plant and animal life. Yes, it is true that those soaps with the biodegradable label are preferred to those that don't have it, however, all soaps do have some impact.

When choosing soaps, look for those that are phosphate free. Keep soap use to a minimum. For personal hygiene carry a cookpot or waterbag full of water two hundred feet away from the nearest water source. Using a bandanna or other small cloth and small amounts of soap, you should be able to sponge-bath easily and rinse completely without polluting the water. A useful item if you care to carry the extra weight and desire a touch of luxury is the shower hose attachment for the 2.5 gallon nylon water bags. They make rinsing off a breeze.

Washing—Pots and Clothing
When washing dishes, utensils, and clothing, soap is not needed. Soap residue can, in fact, cause more harm and discomfort than the odd smudge or speck of dirt. A boiling pot of water is ideal for cleaning and sterilizing dishes and utensils.

Washing clothes can be easily accomplished by holding them in

1

Figure 1-1   The luxury of a shower hose attachment may be worth the extra weight you'll carry.

turbulent water and allowing the natural churning action of the water to clean them. For underwear and socks, heat up a pot of water and clean them away from the stream.

Although scrubbies or steel wool pads are often the first thing most want to reach for when cleaning burned-on food in pots and pans, don't! Cleaning pads accumulate significant amounts of dirt and grime and can become hazardous bacteria breeding grounds in the backcountry. Instead, let the pan or pot soak overnight. Then, sprinkle in a generous amount of sand and grit and, using a bandana or even a clump of dry pine needles, scrub away. Rinse the water into a sump hole and pack out all food residue.

Sump Hole

Although there are those that now consider a sump hole unacceptable, many feel that it remains a far better choice than scattering water with food particles in a wide area around camp. To create a sump hole, dig a hole approximately six inches across and several inches deep. The sump hole must be well away from camp (important in bear country) and at least two hundred feet away from the nearest water source (There are a few exceptions. See Chapters four and five). The hole should be dug in soil that is soft so water will drain easily.

When washing, carefully pour all wash and rinse water into the sump hole. As the water drains down into the soil the food particles will remain trapped at the surface. Before breaking camp, scoop up and pack out all the residue, rinse the hole thoroughly with fresh water and then fill it. Bacteria in the ground will breakdown remaining residuals.

With larger groups, it is better to forego the sump hole because it will not be able to adequately handle the volume of waste and water poured into it. A better alternative is to strain all waste water through a fine-mesh metal screen or strainer back into a pot. Scatter the strained water over a wide area away from camp. The food that is collected in the screen must be either burned or packed out.

Giardia

Although Giardiasis is not fatal, speaking from personal experience, the symptoms are severe enough that many wish it were. The disease is predominantly spread through fecal contamination with water. Although it is rumored that more than 50% of the United States' water is actually pure enough to drink without treatment, the trick is knowing whether or not you are presently drinking some of the pure or contaminated percentage—without sophisticated testing equipment you cannot know! Purify all water or risk the consequences.

All necessary sanitary precautions must be strictly followed or we risk increased contamination of our backcountry waterways.

Human Waste

No method of dealing with human feces in the wilderness is ideal. Latrine, cathole and even surface disposal all have positives and negatives. Contact by animals, insects, and other humans is an inherent problem in disposal of human waste and a chief method of spreading disease.

Improper disposal, no matter what the method, of human feces creates a definite health hazard. Proper disposal does not eliminate health hazards, but it goes a long way in minimizing the risk.

Successful and safe human waste disposal must keep three priorities in mind: prevention of water pollution, or at the very least, minimizing the potential for water pollution; ensuring as rapid and complete a rate of decomposition as possible; prevention of the potential for discovery by and contact with animals or other humans.

Toilet Paper

With the possible exception of an established outhouse, the backcountry user must burn or pack out all toilet paper. Toilet paper will not decompose properly if buried with feces. Be very careful when burning toilet paper—major forest fires have been started by careless campers. It is recommended that you pack out toilet paper during times of extreme fire danger.

Backcountry Outhouses

Outhouses are a traditional solution often provided by park services or other land managers to help cope with waste disposal in high use/impact areas. It can be argued that the potential visual and olfactory shock that may be encountered when coming upon a man-made outhouse in the middle of an otherwise pristine wilderness environment is cause to eliminate outhouses. However distasteful the outhouses may in fact be, an outhouse is often the best alternative to an otherwise unacceptable condition of fields and forests full of little piles and pits of human waste. If an outhouse is made available, use it!

One final word on outhouses: they must never be used for food or trash disposal. That only serves to clog up the outhouse and attract animals.

Surface Disposal

An increasing number of wilderness users advocate surface disposal in desert or high alpine environments. Surface disposal is only appropriate when usage of the area is extremely light and the distance from any water source, including runoff channels, is at least two hundred feet. Select a dry and open area that is blessed with generous amounts of sunlight exposure. Smash, stir and smear your feces to increase the rate of decomposition and its exposure to sun and air.

Catholes

Catholes are often the best way of disposing of human waste

during single night visits to wilderness locations, even when traveling as a group. Unless camping in a highly impacted area, it is best to disperse waste, not concentrate it. While burying does slow decomposition, it minimizes the potential for contact with animals and other humans. The cathole site must be at least two hundred feet from a water source. Choose as level a spot as feasible and dig a hole several inches deep (between 4 to 6 inches) and approximately 6 inches across. Do not dig below the organic layer of soil. When finished, take a stick and stir dirt and feces together to help speed the rate of decomposition. Cover the hole with at least one inch and no more than two inches of top soil.

Latrines

Centralized latrines are the least desirable of all waste disposal methods because of the high degree of impact associated with them,

Figure 1-2 A cathole *must* be at lease 200 feet from a water source.

however, latrines become necessary when disposal sites are limited or if the group stay is longer than one night.

Dig the latrine wider than it is deep—twelve inches in depth is appropriate. Distance the site at least two hundred feet from any water source. Keep a trowel nearby the latrine so, after each use, the feces can be covered by a layer of soil and then compressed with the trowel or boot to accelerate decomposition. Be sure to bury the latrine when it fills to within four inches of the surface soil.

Trash

The real key to successfully dealing with trash in the backcountry is to minimize it from the beginning. Proportion and repackage your food in resealable plastic bags or containers to eliminate cans, bottles, and aluminum foil. By taking the time to accurately proportion your meals, leftovers and trash should be reduced if not eliminated.

"Pack it in, pack it out" is not just the basic motto of those seeking a higher plane and an ideal level of wilderness consciousness. It is the original call for and root of what has become a somewhat sophisticated wilderness ethic. However, despite best intentions and planning, it is very difficult to leave the wilderness carrying all that you came in with. Curious rodents, sudden high winds, or a careless moment all serve to snare a few man-made trophies for mother nature. The trick is to reduce the chances for leaving something behind.

Burnables

The only acceptable burnable trash is paper. Aluminum foil, plastic, and moist food scraps do not burn completely, even in a very hot fire, and leave a residual mess that still must be packed out.

Never place burnables in a cold firepit with the intention of burning them later. Wind, rodents and other animals will only scatter them across the countryside.

Leftover Food

The only practical solution to leftover food is to pack it out, or eat it. Burning usually doesn't work, scattering is unacceptable, and burying food just results in animals digging it up and eventually scattering it anyway. Even worse, animals may suffer by eating food that was never intended for their systems.

Leftover food should be carefully scraped from the cook pot and any other bowls or cups into a resealable plastic bag or container bag. Never allow food to fall into a stream or pond (see Washing under Water Pollution).

Perhaps the only time scattering food particles instead of packing them out is acceptable is with freshly caught fish. Since these animals are indigenous to the area, animals are not likely to have their diets disrupted by eating these scraps. Be sure to scatter the fish remains at least several hundred yards from the campsite so unwanted visitors will not be attracted. Never throw the fish parts back into a stream or lake. The cold water will slow decomposition and the rotting flesh will provide an unsightly and lasting reminder of your visit for months to come.

Special Considerations

Women

Dealing with tampons requires special care. Burying is not a solution as the blood-soaked remains will inevitably be uncovered by digging animals. Burning tampons is often viewed as an unpleasant and sometimes embarrassing task (especially in mixed company) and rarely is the fire hot enough to ensure complete combustion. Packing out the waste is the best solution. Triple bag the tampons in freezer weight resealable plastic bags or container bags for carrying out. There are several ways to minimize odor—especially important when traveling in bear country.

Breaking open a tea bag or crushing an aspirin and sprinkling the leaves or powder over the tampons does help to absorb and hold down the odor. However, the preferred method is burning. Burn the tampons until only charred remains are left. Then pack out the remains—there will be no odor.

Toddlers

For most parents traveling with toddlers, diapers are a necessary evil. With cloth diapers the issue is one of emptying the waste into a cathole and then cleaning and sterilizing the diaper. Boiling water is the best means of sterilization, but consumes large amounts of fuel. Do not use soap when cleaning since it is difficult to rinse out and any soapy residue left in the diaper could cause a serious irritation or rash. Drying can also take some time. Washing of diapers must follow the same standard set out in the section under Water Pollution and Washing.

Many parents, myself included, opt for disposables when in the wilderness. Although bulkier they are more convenient. Burying is never a solution. Empty all waste into a cathole and pack out the remains. To minimize and lighten the load, burn the diaper in a very hot fire until charred remains are left. Pack out what is left—odor free. Because damp diapers are difficult to burn, the combustion process does require an extremely hot fire which in some cases may only partially burn the diaper anyway. Double bag the waste in large garbage bags. Put the garbage bags in a large nylon stuff sack and lash it to the top or outside of your pack. The nylon will prevent tearing and makes an ideal and quick way to tie up the waste with your other garbage when in bear country.

Children

Parents need to be especially mindful of children. Their playfulness and eager energy can sometimes be destructive and disruptive to the environment. This is not to say that one should drastically curb a child's enthusiasm for bounding around outdoors, just that the child must realize certain do's and don'ts.

Teach your children to respect plant and animal life. Children must also be taught (and adults too): Do not break branches; Do not urinate in the water unless park or agency rules established for the wilderness area specifically advise otherwise; Do not drink water without it first being treated. It is also important to help children understand not to throw trash or drop food around camp or on the trails.

Parents will probably have to accompany children when they need to defecate until they are old enough to know how to dig a cathole by themselves and can squat and relax without help. Children must always be required to bring used toilet paper back for burning or have a parent supervise the burning—one careless moment and a forest burns!

Fires

Pros and Cons

While fires of the past were necessary for survival for the most part, this is no longer true today. We cook with stoves, provide light with lanterns and warmth through shelter and clothing. Man may never shake the romantic appeal, however, of a crackling fire deep in the woods under a star flecked sky. For those imbibed with the thrills of adventure, the fire serves as an after-dark elixir—warmly coaxing forward camaraderie, tall tales, and quiet reflections.

But, campfires have a very dark side, more subtle than the scarring forest fires caused by careless builders. Charred fire rings, rocks smudged black from use, scattered coals evident from half-hearted attempts at a wilderness ethic, broken or cut trees and branches, and half burned logs, too large for consumption and left strewn around an abandoned camp are a few of the more obvious impacts. Above all, the most detrimental and long term impact of campfires is the irreversible depletion of natural resources vital for the survival of the ecological balance.

Downed and dead timber is often collected to the point of complete eradication, with campers venturing further and further and depleting more and more. The result is a loss of food and habitat for animals and the elimination of a source of vital nutrients to the soil necessary for continued growth of plants and trees.

Not all campfires are bad however! If camping beside a high alpine lake in the Sierra Nevada of California or White Mountains of New England with limited firewood available, a fire is not a wise choice. When setting up camp deep in the pine forests of the Wind River range of Wyoming or the Cascades of Washington, a properly built fire is a fine addition to the overall experience. Let your common sense guide you.

Keep in mind that a fire, although it adds an essence of romantic warmth, takes away from the potential for a complete nocturnal experience. There is firewood to collect, a fire to clean up, and a dancing light that all but destroys your night vision and obscures the larger world outside the boundaries of the flame.

Firewood Selection

Never cut down trees or branches, living or apparently dead. To do so can cause irreparable harm to the tree, disrupting available habitat for animals; it is illegal in most areas anyway. Leave your saw or axe at home—if you need them, the wood is too large or too green.

Select only wood that is one to two inches in diameter and lying broken on the ground. This wood is more readily consumed by the flames and will result in hotter coals and a better fire for cooking and heating.

Always gather your wood away from camp. This will help to prevent immediate depletion of vital wood resources lying around the camp area.

Only collect what you will use for a relatively small fire. Do not build a giant storehouse of wood as if you are planning on staying the week or winter.

Figure 1-3   First, scrape away duff.

Figure 1-4   Next, create a shallow pit several inches deep and wider than your fire.

One final note, there is no acceptable excuse for building a fire in a new site when a fire ring already exists—even if it is not in the most ideal location.

Construction

Pit

Pit fires should be used only in situations where ground vegetation will not be damaged or where there is no more than just a few inches of underlying duff. The purpose of the pit fire is create a shallow hole where the mineral soil is exposed and the duff is cleared away so that cleanup is easy and the potential for starting a forest fire is eliminated.

First, scrape away all the duff (dead layer of leaves, plants, and needles covering the forest floor) exposing the mineral soil underneath. Clear an area larger than the fire you intend to build. Next, create a shallow pit that is again wider than your fire and several inches deep. Build your fire, but keep it small and efficient.

Mound

Mound fires are ideal when you can find suitable mineral soil that can be dug without disturbing the natural area. Stream beds and sandy areas around boulders are ideal sources for mineral soil.

Choose a large flat rock that is either portable or immobile or

Figure 1-5   Mound Fire

create a rock base by placing two or more relatively flat rocks side-by-side. Next, using a trowel and one of your cook pots, gather soil and spread it at least three inches deep on top of the rock base. Be sure to create a platform that is larger than the area the fire will utilize—2 to 2.5 feet wide is usually enough. Build a small and efficient fire directly on top of the soil.

Fire pan

Although common with river runners, fire pans are gaining in popularity with other wilderness users. Certainly, the prospect of carrying an iron fire pan in a backpack is not an inviting thought, however there are lighter alternatives.

Figure 1-6   The prospect of carrying an iron fire pan in a backpack is not an inviting one.

Perhaps the best way to create a fire pan for backpacking use is with heavy gauge aluminum foil. By laying several three foot long strips side by side with a one inch overlap you will create a very serviceable fire pan. It is also possible to retire an old aluminum space blanket and fold it into a three foot by three foot square. Always cover the aluminum with a several inch thick layer of mineral soil, so the heat will not damage the fire pan. Build a small and efficient fire directly on top of the soil.

Grate

Using a small cooking grate with folding legs will eliminate the need to utilize rocks for securing and supporting cook pots, thereby preventing the scarring of the rocks.

Cleanup

Since it is infinitely more difficult to clean up a fire immediately after you have doused the flames, it is recommended that you do not build a campfire in the morning. That way, no water will be needed to douse the fire and cleanup will be cleaner and faster.

There should be nothing left in the fire but ashes. Refrain from adding additional wood to the flames approximately one hour before finishing the fire. Take the partially burned pieces of larger wood and keep pushing them into the center or hottest coals of the fire. You may find that you need to add very small pieces of wood, twigs and such, to keep the fire hot enough to consume the larger sections of wood.

If you need to add water to douse any embers, do so slowly and sprinkle it on rather than soaking the fire and surrounding soil. Stirring the coals while sprinkling additional water until the embers are out and the fire cold will speed the process. Check the fire for live embers by carefully place your palm near, then on the fire. If you do not sense any warmth, carefully sift through the ashes with your fingers. Again, if you do not feel any warmth, the fire may be declared dead.

Once the fire is cold, all large lumps of charcoal should be crushed. The ashes and crushed charcoal should be spread away from the site leaving no sign of your campfire.

Pick out any food or other trash remnants and pack those out. It is not appropriate to bury or scatter fire-blackened trash with the ashes.

Finally, fill in the pit, scatter the mound, or fold up the fire pan. Rinse off the rock from the mound fire before placing it back in its natural setting. Camouflage evidence of your fire with duff.

If a fire ring was already in existence when you arrived, leave it assembled after cleaning up the ashes and trash. When multiple fire rings are discovered at a single campsite, do the land a favor and dismantle all but one. Fire-blackened rocks should be placed blackened side down and camouflaged. Take the time to carefully scatter the ashes from the dismantled rings and pack out all trash.

Campsites

Qualities of an ideal site

Selection of a campsite and the care of that site are two of the most important aspects to minimum impact travel. A campsite is an area where your use will be concentrated in one small section of wilderness for a comparatively lengthy time. The potential of creating a serious impact on the area, even unwittingly, is high.

When choosing an appropriate campsite, the most important thing you can do is doing nothing to disrupt the natural balance of the wilderness community around you. Moving rocks, digging trenches, cutting trees, and gathering large pieces of dead wood all have a major negative impact on the environment. Seemingly innocent acts such as building a rock wall to shield the wind, damming a creek for swimming, or cutting small branches that are in the way do more than just alter the natural character of the area for the next visitor. All of the above examples make life increasingly difficult for the animals and plants that are dependent on these microhabitats for survival.

If one were to conduct a poll of wilderness travelers regarding the ingredients necessary in an ideal campsite they would probably be as follows: relatively level terrain with generous room for tents and kitchen area; out of the wind; a spectacular view; proximity to water; generous supplies of available deadwood; privacy.

While these are certainly desirable features, not every campsite is going to be the perfect representation of them all. It is never appropriate to "physically alter" a campsite to make it more suitable. John Hart, author of *Walking Softly in the Wilderness*, perhaps sums up ideal campsite selection behavior when he states, "The perfect campsite is found, not made." How true!

Frequency and Type of Use Considerations

Areas of Heavy or Frequent Use

It was once thought that the frequency of campsite use should be kept to an absolute minimum. Established minimum impact policy was to alternate sites in order to prevent overuse and allow each site to recover. Now, however, studies indicate that after several visits, noticeable increase in impact is minimal—the damage having already been done. This would indicate that it is better to limit use of campsites to those areas that are already established. This way, heavy impact of camping sites will be confined to a very small percentage of the wilderness area. It is far better to have significant impact in one or two areas than significant impact in multiple locations.

While it may go against the grain of environmental consciousness to set up camp in an area that is obviously highly impacted with visible trails, tent sites, camp fire ring, and kitchen area, consider that this is the best alternative to subjecting another site to your impact.

Whenever you are presented with a choice of setting up camp in an area that shows a light or moderate impact or in an area that appears overused, choose the area that is most heavily impacted. It is unlikely that any more damage can be done to the heavily affected camp, whereas by not camping in an area that shows light use, you are giving it an opportunity to recover.

Areas of Light or Infrequent Use

For those fortunate enough to be able to travel in pristine wilderness areas, a slightly different approach to campsite selection is appropriate. In these areas, where campsites may not be readily identified and impacts have been kept to a minimum, the wilderness traveler must weigh alternatives carefully and camp in those areas that will show the least amount of immediate or peripheral damage. Sometimes, the prudent choice may be to continue to camp in an area that others have chosen, because this will minimize potential widespread damage.

Location, Location, Location

When selecting where to place your camp, assuming no obvious site exists, there are several important considerations to keep in mind. Duff is preferred to any other surface with vegetative cover, as the impact upon dead leaves and branches is minimal and will show little wear.

An open forest, where generous amounts of light penetrate to the understory is far better than a dense forest when setting up a camp that will impact underlying or nearby vegetation. The sun will encourage a more rapid recovery in an open forest. Dense forests often preserve the visible signs of impact on vegetation and grasses long after the users have gone.

Meadows, previously thought to be the very worst place to camp, are actually an excellent choice if the grass and earth are dry. Recovery of dry meadows where grass is the predominant cover is fairly rapid. Moist meadows are an unquestionably poor choice and should be avoided at all times.

Selecting a Quiet Site

Visual and sound impacts are important considerations when traveling in the wilderness. There are few wilderness travelers that find joy in hiking by a brightly colored camp sitting next to a trail, or in bedding down for the night only able to hear the clamor of a nearby party.

Figure 1-7   An open forest with generous amounts of sun will encourage a more rapid recovery from visible signs of impact.

Be considerate of others and do your best to conceal your camp, visually and audibly. Sound doesn't carry as far among trees as it does across a lake, open meadow, or narrow valley. Consequently, taking the time to set up camp in a timbered area above the valley floor will help to minimize audible disturbance. A benefit to camping above water and the valley floor is that there are usually less mosquitoes, it is typically a few degrees warmer, and it is often more sheltered from the wind. By locating your camp higher on a ridge facing the sunrise, you will be warmed earlier by the sun's rays making drying out or breaking camp even faster and more pleasurable.

Radios or other portable sound devices are as out of place in the wilderness as a billboard. Never camp near a trail or other area that is well traveled by other land users unless it is unavoidable.

Animal considerations

Take local wildlife into account when selecting a tent site. Pitching a tent in the middle of an obvious game trail is asking for trouble—especially if you startle the elk or moose that is used to cruising down an unobstructed path.

Observe that you are not covering animal burrows with a tent or pack. While the tent floor may be viewed as a temporary blockage to a gopher, the ensuing hole in your floor and a rather confused gopher running around in an enclosed tent is not something I would care to wake up to. Other not so pleasant experiences are waking up to a tent covered with ants or a bear sorting through camp—more on the bear in a later chapter.

Figure 1-8 Radios or other portable sound devices are out of place in the wilderness.

Animals are perhaps the best reason to minimize odors and food residue around a camp, especially a regularly used one. Food particles, odors, and the intentional feeding of animals will only serve to attract an unsuitably large and potentially unstable population of animals to the site. Rodents, ants, beetles, flies, various species of bird, and even bears will take to relying on a steady food source from a particular location if it is made available—intentionally or not.

Do not feed the animals, no matter how cute. Take extra care to pick up and pack out all food residue and trash. Do not take food into a tent with you. In bear country, never leave clothing that smells of fish or other cooked food in a tent with you.

Keeping the site pristine

When traveling in lightly used or visited areas, your primary goal is to minimize the impacts made by your presence. This is perhaps most difficult when setting up and breaking down camp.

Both tent dispersal and selection of non-vegetated sites for camping are important when trying to minimize potential impacts. When possible, place the camp on flat rocks, open sandy areas, or snow. This will greatly reduce the opportunity for serious impact of an otherwise untouched and sensitive area.

In a group, spread out the tents, encourage the wearing of soft-soled shoes around camp, keep kitchen and group assembly activities to a minimum, and vary routes to tents, latrine and water. Always be very sensitive to the trampling of vegetation. The use of a water bag or collapsible jug will reduce the number of necessary trips to get water and, consequently, lessen the potential damage.

When staying in any pristine area longer than one or two nights, whether traveling alone or in a group, vary the tent and campsite locations to allow impacted areas an opportunity for recovery.

Finally, just before leaving a site, take time to carefully camouflage impacts. Fluff up compressed vegetation and duff. Disguise scuffed areas with duff and other loose material. Be cautions that you do not over camouflage. You are trying to blend the site into the surroundings, not leave piles of natural litter that look decidedly unnatural.

Hiking impact upon the land

Although there are vast tracts of wilderness areas available to visitors across North America, wilderness users appear to be increasingly conditioned to the idea of easy and ready access. While much of the backcountry gets lightly used, certain trailheads, trail camps, and areas where the fishing or scenery is especially wonderful suffers dramatic overuse. We are in danger of loving selected areas of the wilderness to death.

Consequently, one of the best ways to minimize impact upon the wilderness is to decrease the number of visits to those areas that are subject to heavy overuse. There is so much beauty and special wilderness out there that you will probably be happier for the extra effort and time required to head deeper into or away from heavily used locations.

Using existing trails

Most wilderness travelers seem to prefer to walk on existing trails. That, in itself, is not a problem. Problems occur when the trail is of a poor design, when hikers walk several abreast and widen the trail, when an obstacle blocks the original trail and multitudes of hikers create an alternative trail around the obstacle, or when the wilderness user decides that cutting a switchback is in his best interest.

Minimize impact on existing trails by adhering to a few guidelines. Perhaps the most common impact that can be avoided is not to walk two abreast. Always hike in single file. Walking in a single file helps to prevent damage to the sides of the trail and the potential widening of that trail, or worse—two or more side-by-side paths cutting an ugly swath across a meadow.

Environmental considerations

Mud

Although it may seem somewhat distasteful, walking through the muddy sections of a trail is usually the more suitable alternative to creating an entirely new trail that skirts the problem areas. Waterproof boots and gaitors that prevent water leaking in over your boot-tops are recommended.

Snow

Hiking early in the season often means encountering snow banks that partially or totally cover the trail. Walk across the snowbank if it poses no danger to yourself or the rest of your party. Attempt to create a path across the snow that closely duplicates the route followed by the original trail. That way, when the snow is almost melted, hikers will find themselves on the trail and not walking beside it or in an entirely new location.

Erosion and washed out areas

Sometimes, because of a poorly designed trail or damage caused by unthinking trail users, erosion begins to occur. There is not much you can do in these instances other than walk as carefully as possible across the impacted area, trying to step only on durable and more stable surfaces such as rocks, sand, or snow. Notify the area land manager (or ranger) as soon as possible so that appropriate trail repair measures may be taken. If the problem continues it may become irreparable.

Rest Stops

Often, significant trail damage is done when least expected, during rest stops. Choose rest stops with care. The area selected should be off the trail, out of the way of other users, and on a stable and durable surface such as rock outcroppings or sandy areas. As in a campsite situation, take precautions to minimize damage to surrounding vegetation and soil.

Obstacles

An obstacle on a trail can take many forms, from a fallen tree to other trail users. When encountering others on the trail, either hikers or equestrians, step off the trail and stop. Allow the other group to pass by freely. Do not continue to walk when off the trail as this only results in either widening the trail route or creating an entirely new trail location.

Should you come across a fallen tree or other obstacle, first try to move it. If you are able to move it off the trail without significant damage either to yourself or the trail, then do it. Otherwise, attempt to go over it to prevent establishing an alternative trail. If moving or going over the obstacle is impossible, then carefully select a route around the trail blockage that will minimize lasting impacts. Inform the land manager of the trail blockage so the obstacle can be removed and the alternative trail covered up.

Shortcuts

Shortcutting a switchback in a trail is never a justifiable alternative. These secondary trails, created by selfish and thoughtless trail users, only serve to encourage erosion and scar the land. When coming upon a shortcut, take the time to block it with rocks, small logs, and other brushy debris that may be available. Once again, inform the land manager of the situation and what you have done to help the problem.

Cross-country travel

Although cross-country travel is not for everyone, it is a marvelous way to leave the crowds behind and view a slice of wilderness that few have an opportunity to visit. Cross-country travel is not an alternative for those who cannot travel without leaving a trace. Take only memories and leave only footprints is a generous, though appropriate adage. Preferably one takes only memories and leaves nothing, but that is not always possible.

There are some definite don'ts when heading off the beaten path. Do not blaze trees, do not build cairns or ducks (rocky piles to mark the way), do not leave markers or messages of any sort for others following behind, do not flag branches with flagging tape. Visitors to the wilderness do not belong off the established trails if they cannot navigate without these aids. Do not hike across very wet or swampy meadows.

Keep group sizes small, between 2 to 5 people is appropriate. Plan routes across durable surfaces such as rock, sand, gravel, and snow. Stay off fragile and vegetated surfaces. In an alpine setting, be especially cautions. Many plants, some that are barely visible, have taken years to grow and can be destroyed by the crushing impact of one boot.

In very delicate and fragile areas, such as an alpine environment or tundra, walk only in single file. When even one person's impact creates a visible and significant mark on the land it is better to limit the damage to a single trail which all use.

When hiking across surfaces more durable than alpine soil, spread out. By not following the same route and limiting impact to footprints of one person, the grasses or vegetation will be more likely to recover. Hike in a single file and you risk creating a permanent scar.

Extremely steep or unstable terrain should be skirted unless unavoidable. If at all possible, restrict your ascents and descents on steep slopes to those areas that have snow or rocky areas for you to walk on. Otherwise, the act of digging in your toes or heels will leave highly visible gouges that could lead to significant erosion problems. If you must travel across very steep and unstable or soft soils then spread out. Move carefully and deliberately. Do your best not to dislodge small or large landslides, rocks or other scree. Be cautious that other members of your group are not in the path of falling debris for safety.

Disturbing wildlife

When it comes to traveling in the wilderness, one very important point must be kept in the forefront of your mind; humans are the visitor and the animals the residents. Even though done unwittingly, it is possible to do serious and irreversible harm to feeding habits, breeding behaviors, and nesting habitat if you travel unaware of your potential impact.

Before visiting a particular region, learn about the animals that you will potentially encounter, or at least be sharing the wilderness with. Take extra precautions to ensure that your passing will go relatively unnoticed. A perfect example of this is the High Rock Canyon region in northwestern Nevada. Although the Desert Trail passes through the canyon, the unaware may not realize that the canyon is a vital nesting habitat for raptors from February 15 to April 1 each year. Even the most casual human presence near a nest risks the parents leaving the nest and placing the young in jeopardy of dying.

In other situations, frightened adults may turn tail and run, thinking you are a predator. This alone may not seem significant, but coupled with the possibility that young may be left behind to die, the adults could injure themselves when fleeing, or pregnant females might abort their pregnancy, the potential impact is severe.

Camping near a singular water source for the region, near an animal trail frequently used for nocturnal movement, or near a nest or burrow could cause animals to change their routine which might have a negative impact on their survival rate.

Taking the time to learn about the animals and their habitats will enable you to move quietly and unimpeded without disturbing the wildlife. In return, you will probably have more opportunity to view the magnificence of the wild creatures at a safe distance and from the cover of bushes or rocks.

Respecting solitude and peace

Traveling through the wilderness quietly and unobtrusively is a simple, though often ignored, concept. Yelling, screaming, whistling, bright neon colors, and a me-first attitude are as out of place in the wilds as a shopping mall or housing complex.

It is generally acknowledged by land use managers that most backcountry users visiting wilderness areas are desirous of minimizing contact with other humans. Thankfulness for peace and solitude is the predominant reason many venture into the peaks, valleys and deserts.

Check your attitude and leave it at the trailhead. Enter the wilderness with an eye for appreciation and wonder and a mind for traveling unnoticed by both humans and wildlife. This makes for a more pleasurable journey for both yourself and any others who may happen to share the wilds with you.

2. CAMPGROUND CAMPING

Campground impact

Although campgrounds seem to be the antithesis of wilderness, they often serve as a preferred and excellent base camp for families, photographers, mountain bikers, climbers and many other wilderness seekers desiring a central location from which to day-hike and explore.

While there is nothing wrong with the conveniences many campgrounds offer—showers, country store, grills, picnic tables, play areas for young children, laundry—the impacts associated with a growing number of campgrounds are disconcerting.

Many state and national park campgrounds are becoming nothing more than miniature cities, subject to air pollution, noise pollution, overcrowding, traffic jams and more. Consequently, a consistent campground ethic has become a very important addition to an overall wilderness ethic.

Don't drive when walking is a suitable alternative. This will help alleviate the problems of localized air pollution and traffic congestion. If the country store is only a mile or so away, make a hike of it and leave the vehicle parked. Carry a backpack or sturdy daypack along so that any supplies can be comfortably shouldered back to the campsite.

Figure 2-1 Many state and national park campgrounds are becoming nothing more than miniature cities.

Leave the television and radio at home and consider using ice or propane-power to cool food, thereby eliminating the need to run a generator. Generators are both noisy and polluting.

Don't clean fish, dishes, clothing or yourself in streams or lake water. The problems that are created by these actions in the wilderness are exacerbated in a crowded campground environment to the point of seriously and dangerously polluting the water.

Never feed the wildlife. Feeding the wildlife in a campground area only serves to encourage them to rely on humans as a food source and to forget their natural instincts and fears. This can prove not only dangerous to the animals, but dangerous to humans as well. Watch and wonder, but do not touch and feed. Be extra vigilant with food scraps, cleaning up, and food storage. Many campgrounds have specific rules and provide food storage areas where animals are a potential problem. Follow the rules without deviation.

Figure 2-2 *Never* feed the wildlife. This can prove not only dangerous to the animals, but humans as well.

Figure 2-3   Garbage is a major problem in many campgrounds.

Cutting down trees or using available deadfall wood only serves to completely strip the natural environment around the campground of vital resources. The campground is already impacted sufficiently without campers removing and scarring the trees and wood. Use only wood that is sold by the park or campground for fires—or bring your own.

Do not pick the flowers or plants around the campground. They have a hard enough time surviving as it is, and will only wilt in a few minutes in your hand anyway.

Garbage is a major problem in many campgrounds. I have yet to visit a campground where I can truthfully say the campsite areas were garbage free. Beer bottles, aluminum foil, soda cans, wire hangers, bits of rope, and much more litter many campsites—often thrown thoughtlessly in the firepit. Take the time to pick up carefully around your camping area, and place all trash in available trash receptacles. Sometimes, the trash containers may be full. If this is the case, don't just toss the load on top of the overflowing mess. Find a trash area that is not so full and notify the park management.

Stick to established paths. This is especially important for two reasons. First is the consideration of impact. By staying on the established paths, you are helping to prevent the creation of a ridiculous and unsightly network of trails meandering inevitably nowhere. Secondly, the park often establishes paths with the intention of preserving other campers' privacy. By staying on these established paths, you are minimizing the potential for cutting across another visitor's campsite —definitely not acceptable campground etiquette!

Limit all noise to the boundaries of the campsite, especially at night and in the early morning hours. Loud radios, blaring televisions, rumbling generators, screaming children, obnoxious adults, barking dogs, etc. are the bane of those that are peacefully attempting to enjoy some semblance of wilderness sanctity.

3. LAKES AND RIVERS

Special concerns

Use of a vast and available network of waterways to explore the backcountry is on the rise, almost to the point of becoming a problem in some areas. For families and many others, utilizing water trails has become a very safe and accessible means of enjoying and sharing the wilderness. Unfortunately, as our demand for water by-ways increases, their availability decreases, often due to drought, dams, and irrigation diversions.

Unlike other wilderness areas, the banks of rivers, oceans and lakes offer a relatively durable camping environment if cared for properly. Even though the river or lakeside environment is typically more resilient, we must take great pains not to impact it more than necessary.

Repeated visitations and limited camping locations serve to concentrate use to a narrow strip of land beside a river or lake. Although water ways often are able to cleanse themselves with annual flooding or high water and vegetative recovery is often more rapid by the water's edge, overuse and constant abuse can cause irreparable harm. Because of a river's durable nature, once damaged it becomes much harder to repair.

Campsite selection

Wherever you choose to spend the night, do so below the high water line if at all possible. Whenever the river floods or the water level rises, all traces of your camp will be erased and the area restored to its virgin state for the next visitor to enjoy. Camping beyond the highwater line will create impacts that are not easily removed. Keep in mind that on many dam-controlled rivers, camping below the high water line may not be possible or wise as daily water releases may raise the water level regularly.

If you must camp above the high water line, do so out of view of other river users and on a durable site. Most often, especially if the river or lake is a popular destination, there will already be several impacted sites from which to choose. Frequently, in these highly impacted areas, state and federal agencies require camping away from the river or lake edge. Do not make a new site, use the ones already in existence.

Wildlife and plants

A river or lake is an artery of life-giving moisture to the area and its inhabitants. Do not hamper the flow of life by obstructing animal's

Figure 3-1   Camp below the highest water line if at all possible.

paths, by carelessly trampling or cutting vegetation, or in any way disturbing the natural order. Camp away from dens, feeding grounds, obvious watering holes and do your best to remain only an observer to the river and its domain.

Water pollution

Although it may be tempting, resist any urge to bathe directly in the water. All personal cleansing should be performed at least two hundred feet away from the nearest water source. Taking an initial dip to wet yourself prior to soaping up is all right. However, all rinsing must be done two hundred feet away from the water's edge with a bucket.

Waste water from cooking or cleaning pots (providing no soap was used) should be dumped directly into the river or lake. First, pour the waste water through a bandana or other fine cloth to remove any solid food particles and as much residual oil as possible. Bag all the particles in a resealable plastic bag or other trash receptacle. Wade out away from the immediate edge (maintain a definite margin of safety when doing this) and pour the thoroughly filtered waste water directly into the flow of the river or away from the lake shore. The old practice of scattering waste water around the camp only serves to attract flies, other insects and rodents. Additionally, the odor during hot months can become quite intolerable.

Figure 3-2 Pour waste water through a fine cloth to remove solid food particles, and bag the pieces in a trash receptacle.

Campfires

The building of campfires in any riparian environment dictates the mandatory use of a fire pan. Barbecue grills, steel baking pans, and garbage can lids all make excellent fire pans. All ashes and other charred remains from a fire must be carried out. Designate a large surplus ammo can for this purpose. Each night, place the previous night's ashes from the can in the bottom of the fire pan and build the new fire over them. By doing this you will continue to reduce the collective volume of the ashes and charcoal as much as possible. Dumping ashes and charcoal in the river or lake, or scattering them around the shoreline is not a suitable practice.

Increasingly, rivers and lake shores are being stripped of available wood, even driftwood. In fact, many popular river campsites are already bare. Because of this, it is recommended that you pack your own wood supply and supplement it with charcoal for cooking purposes. Either that or use a stove; the choice is yours.

Human waste

There are those who argue that urinating directly into the river or lake is a defensible practice. With increase education, however, we have come to realize that urine is not the sterile liquid we once thought, and that it may, in fact, harbor resistant organisms that lead to disease. Urinating directly in water ways is not acceptable under any circumstances (although some state and federal agencies continue to advocate this method in their established rules for river use), not with the volume of use our rivers and lakes now see. Urinate as far away from the camp and water source as possible.

Disposal of feces requires the use of a portable toilet. An excellent river toilet can be made by purchasing a large waterproof surplus ammunition can and lining it with several heavy-duty garbage bags, folded over the rim. Place a toilet seat on the top (with the lid open of course) for a pleasurable throne. Use a sprinkling of bleach or quicklime to help keep odors down and minimize the production of methane gas which could lead to an embarrassing explosion once the bag is sealed.

Deposit all toilet paper directly into the can along with the feces. Do not urinate in the can as this only makes handling of the can sloppy and dilutes the chemicals, limiting their effectiveness. Keep the box covered with an extra bag to help minimize the attraction to flies between uses. Before packing up each day, squeeze the air out of the bag, then close and store it in the same box.

Figure 3-3   The top-of-the-line in pleasurable wilderness thrones…

Trash

Anything that is not burnable must be carried out. Food scraps are often the greatest problem on beach campsites. Leftover food not picked up attracts insects and rodents in droves. Minimize this by spreading out a durable tarp that will be used as a floor and boundary for the eating area. All meals must be served and eaten on this tarp. Then, after each meal, the scraps are easily picked up and packed out.

Bank Erosion

Recently, research has shown that dragging boats up and down river banks as well as walking from camp to the river to obtain water is a leading source of bank erosion. While it is not possible to completely eliminate river bank impacts, river users must begin to take extreme steps to minimize impacts that can lead to banks collapsing or becoming irreversibly scarred.

Whenever possible, choose expansive beaches or other areas which facilitate access to the water without having to negotiate steep and easily eroded banks.

4. DESERTS

Special concerns

From a distance, the desert appears foreboding and stark to many people. Its blowing sands and arid soil appear lifeless. The desert is a study in contrasts; apparently lifeless and yet very much alive, hardy and at the same time fragile.

Traveling through a desert environment requires a special sensitivity and awareness. While many plants are more resistant to harm because of their thorns and thick skins, once damaged they are unlikely to recover.

Fragile soils

Cryptogamic soils are distinctive to desert and certain desert/riparian environments. Made up of a very thin layer of usually dark mineral soil on top and an underlying layer of mosses, lichen, algae, and fungus, cryptogamic soils form a unique biological unit that represents an initial and very tenuous foothold for future plant communities. Viewed closely, cryptogamic soil gardens resemble a moonscape with jagged, upraised towers and craters.

The cryptogamic soil plays a critical role in providing erosion prevention and helping to create a nutrient-rich base upon which more substantive plant communities can thrive. While this soil takes almost a hundred years to form, it only takes a few seconds and several footprints to wipe it out—turn it to dust.

Where existing trails are evident in desert environments, use them. Do not deviate from the trail except on durable surfaces such as slickrock. In areas where trails do not exist, hike in a single file line and limit your impact to a narrow strip across the desert's surface.

Camping

Finding established campsites in the desert is often impossible because of the high rate of recovery from desert plants that resist trampling and sandy or rocky terrain that shows little wear. Still, campsites must be selected with care and with an attitude similar to that of previously discussed pristine sites.

Choose areas that are relatively free from vegetation and on a durable surface such as a dry wash, slickrock or any other terrain free from cryptogamic soil. To further minimize impact potential, it is important to keep group sizes small and the length of overnight stays to a minimum.

Campfires

Stoves only is the primary rule of thumb in the desert. Because of the low production of woody material in the desert, whatever vegetation may be available for burning is critically needed for nutrient cycling.

Upon occasion, you may happen across a desert wash where abundant driftwood, left over from the last heavy rains and floods, sits piled up. This is perhaps the only time where fires may be considered suitable. Since most desert washes are predominantly mineral soil, their location is ideal for campfires—no rocks to blacken. Just create a shallow pit and cover it in the morning. Be sure to grind up all charcoal bits and scatter the ashes and particles to the wind before departing.

Sanitation

In the desert, it is especially critical that you defecate, urinate and wash as far away from potential water sources as possible—arroyos, gullies, and shallow soil on rocky surfaces. The presence of microorganisms in desert soil is minimal, which serves to maximize the length of time needed to break down solids such as human feces.

While some advocate surface defecation, this is only acceptable in areas where the possibility for human contact is minimal. Unlike in forest and moist climates, insect and animal contact is not a problem, however, visual contact still is. Feces left on the surface remain for a considerable amount of time due to the arid nature of the surroundings.

Catholes are the preferred choice, but they differ slightly from those dug in moister environments. The goal is to bury feces just below the surface with enough soil cover to prevent visual discovery but not enough to prevent the sun's heat from destroying pathogens and aiding in the breakdown.

Group latrines are not appropriate in desert environments because of the fact that microorganisms are few and deep burial only serves to preserve the feces in a cool and protected tomb for many years to come.

Water

Water sources in the desert are minimal, and those that do exist must be protected diligently, almost obsessively. Never camp near a water source, no matter how tempting. Your presence near a vital desert water source may drive wildlife away that is depending upon that water for survival.

Conserve all water sources. Keep personal washing, clothes washing, and dish washing to an absolute minimum. Always use a clean cup or pot to scoop water from the source. Oily or grimy hands

Figure 4-1 One careless move could collapse a natural dam.

or dirty containers could carry contaminants that will remain in the water source for a long time. Frequently, bowls or miniature springs are only full of water by chance and one careless move could collapse a natural dam, fill the bowl with dirt and sand, or block the underground water source. Move deliberately and carefully around any water sources.

Artifacts

It is not unusual to come across Indian artifacts when traveling through desert environments. Anasazi ruins dot the Southwest and periodically burial sites or other buildings are located—even in backyards buried under centuries of earth. Unfortunately, the vast majority of these precious sites have been and continue to be defiled and vandalized by people who deserve no more recognition than to be called immoral and mindless idiots.

If you happen upon an ancient dwelling in your wanderings treat it with the respect that it deserves. Explore them only with great care and reverence. Revel in the silence and religious experience of another culture's history—take nothing with you, leave nothing behind.

5. AMPHIBIOUS CANYONEERING

A Most Delicate Environment

Standing waist deep in water while staring up at a 1,000-pound log wedged in the narrow canyon walls above your head may not give the impression of traveling through a fragile and irreplaceable environment. On the contrary, the rugged nature of and difficulty presented by traveling through remote riparian canyons in Utah and Arizona presents a picture of a magnificent yet unforgiving and potentially violent offering. Yet, these amphibious canyons demand the highest level of wilderness ethic. Once polluted or vandalized, their resources and beauty are irreplaceable.

Traveling Through

Much of your travel through canyons of this nature will be in the form of raftpacking—floating your pack along the streambed and pulling or pushing it. Only travel in small groups. Any group larger than four is too large and the resulting impacts will be severe.

Do not bring pets along. Although some will argue that properly controlled dogs have a place in the wilderness for comfort and pleasure reasons, amphibious canyoneering is not one of those places. The intensity of swimming, jumping, climbing, and rough scrambling will not be a pleasure for either the dog or yourself.

Always stay in the streambed unless circumstances force you out. Bushwacking along the lush edges of a these canyon-bottom, riparian

Figure 5-1   Once polluted or vandalized, amphibious canyons permanently loose their beauty and resources.

environments will cause permanent damage both to the delicate soil structure (cryptogamic soil for you naturalists) and the vegetation. Do not pick or even touch the flowers.

On occasion, traveling through certain sections of a canyon will require you to use climbing ropes, slings, and anchors. It is not a reasonable practice to leave behind an anchor, rope, or sling. If you cannot take your equipment with you, then do not use it. Find an alternate method or route.

Sanitation

It is a difficult process, but do your best to refrain from sending wastewater directly into the stream. It is virtually impossible to practice washing and urination two hundred feet from many canyon-bottom streams. At least attempt to provide as much filtration opportunity as possible by dumping wastewater in the soil, rocks, and sandy environs away from the immediate stream edge. Adequately filter all wastewater through a bandana so that all food and particulate matter is removed before dumping it. Pack out all solid waste.

Boater's rules should apply in regards to defecation. Create a miniature river-runner's toilet using a coffee-can lined with multiple plastic bags. Add small amounts of chlorine bleach to prevent odor

Figure 5-2 The do-it-yourself miniature river-runner's toilet kit.

and gas production. Do not urinate in the bags. Squeeze out all air when packing, seal the bags, and then replace the coffee-can lid to secure the contents.

Camping

Camp only on sand banks, gravel washes, or rocky ledges. Never set up camp in vegetated areas. Campfires are not acceptable, even with significant amounts of driftwood littering the canyon. The resulting blackening of rocks and ash/charcoal production leaves behind permanent reminders of your visit. Stoves are the only environmentally sound way of cooking.

6. COASTLINES

Defining singular special considerations for coastlines is fraught with exception and variance. What is acceptable on a Vancouver Island coast may cause problems on a Baja coast. What is defined as high impact on a Nova Scotia coast may be considered preferred practice in the Gulf of Mexico. Coastlines around the world vary measurably from being considered rainforests to deserts to wetlands to arctic tundra.

Despite the differences, there are some generalizations that can be made regarding travel and exploration of coastline environments. At times adaptation and modification of the generalizations is called for. Use your common sense and best judgement in all cases.

Coastal environments are generally the most resilient and recoverable of all the wilderness areas you may choose to visit. The regular flooding and churning action of high tides and storms acts as a highly effective cleanser, stripping impacts and rapidly returning beaches and coasts to a pristine state. This is not a license to drop your vigilance regarding minimum impact though, because inland from these hardy coastlines lie extremely sensitive ecosystems that are easily disrupted and scarred. Moreover, although impacts upon the intertidal zones of many coasts may be washed away with regularity, where are they being washed away to? It is foolhardy to imagine that they just disappear.

41

Campsites

Within the upper reaches of intertidal zones (areas of the beach that are alternately covered by water and exposed to air) exists a strip of land that is devoid of vegetation and organic soil, yet is flooded only once monthly by the highest tides. It is on this strip of land that setting up camp is most ideal.

Gone is the worry of traffic lanes and closely packed tents and cooking areas as long as all activity is limited to this particular strip of coast. Once a month the tides will come and wash the beach clean of all visible impacts—do not camp in the intertidal zone during this time.

If you simply cannot time your visit to miss the monthly high tides, then selection of a campsite becomes much more discriminating. Find a site that has already been impacted, select the most resilient area, and maintain the camp in a manner described previously for pristine camps. Do not locate your camp upon relatively new sand dunes with little or delicate vegetation. Areas covered with grasses that are well established are a preferred location as the grasses are usually more resistant to trampling. Any significant impact upon the sands and coasts immediately above the areas of highest tides will encourage wind and rain erosion, which could prove disastrous in the long term.

Figure 6-1   The intertidal zone is the most ideal place to camp when it is not high tide month.

Fires

In areas where driftwood is abundant, campfires are perfectly acceptable. Do use caution when rummaging through driftwood in certain areas, as often these wood piles are prime habitats for rattlesnakes. Build your campfire on mineral soil within the daily intertidal zone, so all evidence of your presence will be washed away quickly. In areas where there is heavy use, crush all charcoal to speed the cleansing process.

Standard campfire rules continue to apply regarding wood selection and use. It is not appropriate to gather large amounts of wood for stockpiling nor is it desirable to build massive blazes or use wood that will only partially be consumed. Build only small, efficient fires that meet basic cooking and warmth needs. Smaller fires are more easily washed away and disguised when you leave.

Sanitation

Because of the regular cleansing action of the tides and the high bacteria count common within the intertidal zones, dealing with human waste is somewhat easier. Urination is best done in the lower reaches of the intertidal zone where daily tide action will wash the beach and flush the contaminants away.

Standard catholes work quite efficiently along coastlines because of the higher moisture and microorganism content of the organic soils above the tide zones. In more remote locations where visitation is light, it is acceptable to defecate on the surface where the daily tide will come and wash the feces away. The high bacteria count and wave action are very efficient at breaking down human waste quickly. An alternative method used by some is to defecate on a flat rock and then toss the rock directly into the surf. This choice is fine as long as the area is a remote one and sees light use—watch where you aim!

Whether urinating or defecating, stay away from tide pools since tide pools are very sensitive to water pollution, and the wave action may not clean them out as vigorously or completely as is required.

Waste disposal

The disposal of solid waste is simple; pack it in, pack it out. Cans, bottles, aluminum foil, and all other nonburnable items should be carried until they can be properly disposed of.

Small amounts of leftover food are best disposed of by scattering them well offshore where scavenging birds and other animals will consume them. Large amounts of leftovers should be saved for

Figure 6-2   Pour wash water directly into the sand within the daily intertidal zone.

consumption later or packed out along with the nonburnables. In areas where bears could be considered a problem, burn the food to destroy odor, and then pack out the remaining residue.

Wash water and cooking water should be poured directly into the sand or gravel within the daily intertidal zone. The wave action will cleanse the area and break up the waste. Do not pour waste water directly on the ocean. This often results in creating an ugly film that is more difficult for the surf to break down.

Wildlife impact

Coastlines are a particularly rich environment full of wildlife. Often, this wildlife uses the coastline to breed, for protection during migration, or for exclusive feeding habitat. Consequently, any visit to remote shores and islands carries with it a responsibility to take extreme precautions towards minimizing contact with wildlife.

Avoid beaches that are being used as a nesting area or rookery. Studies have shown that a human presence can cause severe impacts upon breeding and nesting animal populations. Frightened birds fly away leaving nests unprotected against predation. Seals and sea lions have been known to stampede in panic, trampling and crushing young in their desperate surge for the sea.

Photograph and observe all wildlife only from a protected distance, upwind and concealed from view. At any sign of uneasiness, back away carefully and do not return.

If you are supplementing your diet with seafood, do so carefully and conservatively. Take only what you need and limit your catch to males when catching lobster or crab—although that is sometimes difficult since identification of sex is often a challenge even for experts (females are often carrying eggs that ensure the future of the species). Harvesting shellfish must be done with care. Do not deplete populations and do not harvest in areas where shellfish are not in abundance.

7. SNOW AND ICE

Nordic or cross-country skiing and a mild resurgence of snowshoeing has served to popularize backcountry winter travel and camping. The purity and peace of a winter wonderland laden with snow is a magical experience. Because much of the land lies under a cloak of snow and ice, many immediate impacts often associated with wilderness travel are minimized or virtually eliminated.

Damages to underlying soils and vegetation are prevented by the cushion of snow. Travel and camping impacts are often quickly concealed under a mantle of new-fallen snow. Bright clothing, often discouraged in warmer months, is preferred for reasons of safety. Fewer visitors also minimizes the possibility of paths crossing and the associated visual and audible impacts upon other users.

What impacts remain are made more serious by the very harshness and cold of the winter. Waste does not deteriorate, wet soils during seasonal melts are easily impacted, and spring plants remain trapped under a thin coating of packed and hardened snow. Wildlife, struggling for survival with limited food resources and restricted movements, become more stressed by human contact.

Wildlife impact

During the winter months, the wildlife that remains and does not migrate to lower elevations or warmer climates suffer severe and often debilitating impacts from winter recreationists—snowshoers, cross-country skiers, snowmobilers.

Figure 7-1 It is impossible to predict how an animal will react to your presence.

Many animals have difficulty finding available food sources, and because these animals must conserve energy to stay warm, they restrict their movements to searching for food and escaping danger. This is most critical with larger mammals such as elk and deer. When humans approach, the danger mechanism is triggered often driving the animal into an exhausting attempt to escape. For weakened animals that are clinging to life, this action may result in death.

Always use extreme caution when near wildlife. It is best to keep at least two hundred yards between yourself and the animal or animal herd. Since it is often impossible to predict how an animal will react to your presence, keep a close watch and withdraw at the first sign of agitation.

It is especially important that you do not camp near winter feeding, watering, or bedding areas. To do so will only drive the animals away from vital and already minimal sources of shelter and food.

Sanitation

Urinate at least two hundred yards away from present and future water sources—a frozen lake surface is not a good location. Since yellow snow is unsightly, take the time to cover it with a light coating of snow.

Because of the cold temperatures, feces will not deteriorate easily. Surface deposition is appropriate only when others will not come into contact with the human waste. A shallow cathole is often the preferred choice. In either case, since the feces will likely end up sitting on the soil after the spring thaw, select an area where future human contact is likely to be avoided. A dense grove of trees on a slope or in snow lying above dense shrubbery are good choices as it is unlikely that others will choose those sites for a camp during the spring or summer. Also, defecate well away from present and future water sources—defecating in the bottom of an established runoff gully to the nearby lake is not appropriate.

In popular areas where the snow remains year-round, latrines are the only environmentally sound solution. In a cold environment where decomposition is limited it is far better to concentrate feces in one location than to scatter it liberally around the campsite. In remote or lightly visited areas, surface defecation or shallow catholes are appropriate. As always, when traveling within national, state or other park boundaries, practice winter waste disposal according to each park's particular guidelines.

Figure 7-2   To dispose of feces, select an area where human contact is likely to be avoided.

Trash

Snow makes the handling of trash more difficult, hiding or disguising it from view and then dumping it unceremoniously on the soils for others to discover after the spring thaw. Ski wax, plastic, white rope, toilet paper, white candles, cellophane candy wrappers, white dental floss, and more disappear into the white veil almost magically. Even the most diligent and environmentally conscious winter traveler finds it hard to keep track of his or her trash.

One solution is to carry only brightly colored gear. Colored dental floss, colored candles, colored rope—you get the idea. Toilet paper literally refuses to burn in the snow often leaving a white, soggy mess to either be packed out or discovered unpleasantly by others later. Almost surprisingly, snow makes a wonderful substitute for toilet paper, and despite the initial cold shock upon application, it cleans gently and easily. Even more ideal is the fact that snow disappears during a melt, leaving no residual evidence.

Waste water should be dumped away from camp and potential water sources. Use a sump hole and pack out all food particles when breaking camp.

Campfires

Although it can be argued that campfires leave little or no trace when properly constructed on snow or ice, they are not a suitable alternative from a strictly minimum impact point-of-view and should only be used in emergencies. Wood is often scarce and frequently wet, leading fire builders to strip small branches from available trees— definitely not proper. Additionally, ashes and coals are virtually impossible to dispose of properly in the snow and often leave behind a soggy and unattractive pile of sludge come spring.

Spring thaw

A tremendous amount of damage may be inflicted on trails and meadows during the thaw because everything is wet. In these conditions, stick diligently to trails, even if muddy. Be extremely cautious that you do not create new or alternative routes across meadows. Camp in areas that are driest and most resistant to impacts— preferably still on snow.

Figure 7-3 Snow hides trash from view until spring comes to thaw it out.

8. BEARS AND OTHER ANIMAL CONSIDERATIONS

Bears

Bears, like humans, are omnivorous, which means they eat anything made available to them. Because of this and because of their size, they present a potential opportunistic hazard to humans. This does not imply that bears should invoke a panic attack whenever nearby, just that they should be respected and proper precautions taken to protect them and us.

Black Bear

Although black bears will typically run when threatened, there have been quite a significant number of attacks recorded over the years. Primarily, these attacks appear to occur in areas where the bear has become habituated to human contact and food. Fortunately, most of the injuries recorded were minor.

Black bears are especially opportunistic and are quite resourceful at acquiring the skills necessary to obtain food. One ranger reported a mother sending her cubs up trees and out onto the branches campers were using to hang food. There they would bounce and crawl even further out on each branch until it broke, tumbling food and cubs to the ground in a confused heap and tangle. While the mother bear gets no points for being a good parent, she does get points for ingenuity.

It is important to remember that bears are attracted to odor—fish, perfumed soap, deodorant, etc. Conceal the odor and you greatly reduce the possibility of attracting a bear's attention. Hang your food using the counterbalance method described below.

Place all items of food and other items that carry a strong odor (toothpaste, trash, soap, deodorant) into two equally weighted bags. The bags should be lined with plastic garbage sacks to help conceal odors. Select a branch that is at least 4 inches in diameter at its widest point and approximately 20 feet off the ground.

Weight one end of a fifty foot rope and toss it over the branch approximately 10 feet from the trunk. It is important that the branch be strong enough to support the bags of food, but not strong enough to support bear cubs—discouraging them from edging out and dislodging the rope.

Hoist one bag all the way to the top so it is touching the branch. Tie the other bag as high on the rope as possible, leaving a loop large enough so that it can be easily hooked by a long stick when you want to pull the bags down.

Using a sturdy stick, push the second bag upwards. Since the bags are counterbalanced the other bag should descend. Stop when both bags are hanging side-by-side. Both bags should hang approximately 10 to 12 feet above the ground.

Figure 8-1   It is important to remember bears are attracted to odor.

Figure 8-2a   When going to hang food, select a branch at least 4 inches in diameter, and about 20 feet from the ground.

Figure 8-2b   Hoist one bag all the way to the top so it touches the branch.

Figure 8-2c   Tie the other bag as high as possible, leaving a loop large enough so it can be easily hooked with a stick.

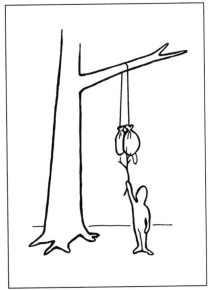

Figure 8-2d   Using a large stick, push the second bag upwards.

Figure 8-3   Keep the rope approximately 10 feet from the trunk. It should be strong enough to support the food, while being discouraging to a heavy bear cub.

To retrieve the bags, hook the loop that you tied in the rope with a long stick and pull one bag towards you. Sometimes you may have to push one while pulling the other.

In general, if you keep your camp clean, you should experience no serious bear problems. A bear may still periodically attempt to wander through just because you are on his selected route for the evening. If a bear should happen to approach your camp, yell, bang pots, wave your arms, and the bear should retreat. If the bear doesn't retreat, you should.

Use a certain amount of caution when trying to drive off a bear. Recently, a group of Yosemite campers I came across shared a bear adventure they had experienced. Two cubs wandered into camp. Thinking they had better drive the little ones off lest mom follow, they set about yelling and banging. The two cubs shot straight up the nearest tree—in the middle of camp—and set off the alarm by bawling their heads off. Mom came running and the campers scattered. Five hours later, the cubs finally got the nerve to come down and wander off with mom. Six hungry campers slunk back into camp and went to bed. The moral of the story is: nothing is ever cut and dry in the wilderness.

Never take food or clothing that smells of food into a tent. Bears are a curious sort and will rip and tear through fabric if potential food is smelled. Imagine the surprise of a bear rummaging through a tent door only to find a human and not food. In a conflict between a bear and a human, the soft-skinned human will inevitably come out the worse for wear initially. In the long run, once a bear attacks a human, no matter who is at fault, the bear is either removed from the area or put to sleep—an ultimate losing proposition.

Brown Bear—Grizzly and Alaskan

Grizzly bears and Alaskan brown bears are probably more feared by humans because they are larger, more aggressive, and apparently more unpredictable than their cousins the black bear.

In addition to the precautions listed for black bears, grizzly bears require increased vigilance and caution if contact is to be minimized. Although there is a lot of conflicting evidence offered by seeming experts and government agencies, the most sound advice appears to come from Doug Peacock in an October 1990 *Backpacker Magazine* article, "Hiking Safely in Grizzly Land." Doug Peacock speaks with proven authority having spent most of each summer and fall for twenty years backpacking and tenting in grizzly habitat. A word of caution though. Even Mr. Peacock admits that his word is not gospel and that grizzlies are an unpredictable sort—but then that is why they are called wild animals.

According to Mr. Peacock, when moving down a trail stop, listen every five minutes or so for bear. Travel quietly. Stay alert and see the grizzly before he sees you. If confronted, do not run and do not try to climb a tree. Retreat gracefully if possible when the grizzly has his head down or turned to the side. If the grizzly looks right at you, raise your arms, keep your head turned to one side and speak to it so it knows what you are. Avoid mother grizzlies since they are considered the most dangerous. Again, if confronted stand your ground. Running will invite a charge, and if you keep running, an attack. Watch for carcasses. Grizzlies cache their food and remain relatively near it until it is consumed. Never pitch your tent in subalpine meadows, along drainages, in saddles, or on ridges gentle enough to encourage bear travel. Bears frequent trails too, so if caught out at night, set up camp as far away from a trail as possible. Sleep in a tent regardless of weather, and sleep away from the sides. No guns—they'll just get you into more trouble. No bear repellents—ditto the gun advice. Don't drop your pack when confronted by a grizzly. If the pack distracts him, you weren't in danger of being attacked in the first place. Worse, your food in the pack is likely to corrupt him and endanger the next hiker.

Rodents, etc.

Though rodents, skunks, foxes, or raccoons certainly don't present the same threat bears do, they can create a world of trouble if allowed. Like bears, most animals are attracted to food and will seek it out wherever it may be. An expensive pack, a tent wall, a fanny pack; they are all the same to an animal if food is contained within—something that must be chewed through or torn apart to get at the goodies.

As in bear country, take no food to bed. Empty all food out of your pack. Store food in a bag hanging above ground and out of reach of rodents or raccoons. Leave all pockets to your pack open—a rodent or raccoon will often use the easiest entrance if invited, or the most difficult if blocked. While a chewed pocket may not seem serious, I have heard of rodents chewing right through a pack, rendering it virtually useless for carrying anything except a sleeping bag and tent.

Figure 8-4   It is best to simply leave all the pockets of your pack open.

9. MOUNTAIN BIKING

A New Kind of Impact

It can be argued fairly convincingly that under normal conditions mountain bikes present no more of an environmental impact risk than do other trail users. Certainly, in some instances equestrian use serves to rototill the land and does far more damage than a mountain bike ever could. However, the potential for reckless mountain bike use to do serious environmental damage is beyond debate. When was the last time you saw a hiker kicking up a spray of dirt in a power skid?

While it appears as if most mountain bikers are responsible users, there is a small contingent that repeatedly tear up existing trails, create new trails, and scatter other trail users in a malicious demonstration of ultimate irresponsibility.

Because mountain bikes can glide over trails with speed, efficiency, and relative silence, the possibility for trail use conflicts is enhanced. Too much speed combined with a blind corner on a trail could result in either a nasty collision or a heart-stopping scare for equestrians or hikers out for a quiet stroll. One acquaintance wears a small cow-bell that tastefully and repeatedly announces his presence several hundred feet before possible encounters with other trail users. Hikers and equestrians alike have thanked him for his thoughtfulness, and his control.

Figure 9-1   Watch your speed on the trail when your vision is limited.

Speed and Conflict

If you feel the need for speed, then save it for a race. Nobody enjoys being blasted off the trail by a subsonic mountain bike. Practicing high-speed descents and training for races can be accomplished by riding in little used areas with caution or on private land with landowner permission. Never ride on private land or in closed areas. This will result in only enhancing the negative image many share towards mountain biking.

When approaching hikers or equestrians, yield the right-of-way. Pull over to the side of the trail and stop. Adopt a friendly manner. If the hiking party chooses to move off the trail for you, thank them and ride by very slowly.   Whenever pulling off the trail, do so without damaging sensitive vegetation along the trail's edge. If you come up behind other trail users, slow to their pace and then call out gently for permission to pass. When that permission is granted, wait for a wide enough area so that you do not widen the path when riding by.

It is never warranted to ride fast in popular hiking or equestrian areas. When riding in areas that receive heavier usage, keep speeds slow and deliberate, always riding in tight control of your bike when on descents and flat stretches.

Terrain considerations

There will be some moments when it is not appropriate to ride on a particular section of trail, even if it is marked as open. Very muddy or wet sections of a trail are extremely sensitive to the channeling affect of a mountain bike's tires and the potential gouging and tearing that may occur on corners, difficult ascents, and steep descents. If most of the trail is dry, but you encounter a few very wet sections, dismount and carry your bike over those sections. Remember to stay on the trail, though, and do not create another path. Wet feet are a far better choice than creating another erosional path.

Locking up the brakes during a downhill is perhaps one of the most damaging things a mountain biker can do to the trail. The studded tires will gouge and tear the trail in most instances and can begin to create ugly channels and chewed up earth that is more susceptible to erosion.

Figure 9-2 Locking your brakes while going down a hill can be most damaging to a trail.

Never leave the trail for any reason. Hills are easily scarred by the wayward wanderings of a few renegade mountain bikers and resulting paths often lead to major erosion problems. Where one biker goes, others are sure to follow. Try to obscure or block illegal trails if at all possible.

If you encounter an obstacle in the trail, first try to move it. If that doesn't work then attempt to ride over it, and finally, if you have no other choice, get off your bike and carry it around the blockage. Remember to inform the ranger or land manager of the obstacle.

Wildlife

Afford wildlife the same consideration you do other trail users. Refrain from riding up quickly behind them or scattering a herd with a sharp yell. This is especially important with domestic herds, such as cows, as they are easily spooked and the resulting stampede could cause serious harm to the herd and, potentially, to other trail users.

A mountain bike's place

As an avid mountain biker myself, I feel that I can speak with a certain objective authority on the right of mountain bikers to ride where they please. In terms of physical impact upon the land, studies have shown that mountain bikes leave no more trace than other users in most cases. However, in terms of intruding upon the sanctity of pure wilderness and the right of others to use it without fear of a mechanical devise bearing down on them, mountain bikes become an entirely different issue.

It is my decided opinion (although I do reserve the right to amend it at any time) that whether cruising the single tracks or fire roads, responsible mountain bikers have as much right to use nonwilderness designated public lands as anyone. In protected wilderness areas, however, mountain bikes should not be allowed.

As a fellow mountain biker and author Michael McCoy said in a 1990 *Trilogy Magazine* article, "Mountain bikes are an efficient and fun means of getting out into nature and exploring the outdoors. But the wilderness doesn't need mountain bikes, and mountain bikers don't need the wilderness. Wilderness is for leaving behind our high-tech gadgetry and slowing down our need-for-speed temperaments. Moreover, wilderness areas exist for the protection of ecosystems —do not disturb zones for the plants and animals that have no say in what man does to the rest of the planet."

I couldn't have said it any better myself. The Wilderness Act of 1964 states that within those lands protected as wilderness areas, "there shall be no . . . use of motor vehicles . . . no other forms of mechanical transport." End of discussion.

Figure 9-3 The Wilderness Act of 1964: "there shall be no...use of motor vehicles...no other forms of mechanical transportations."

10. CLIMBING

Climbing, in its purest form, does little to impact the land. Gone is the frequent use of pitons, scarring and breaking the rock needlessly. Instead, most climbers resort to removeable protection and often take great care not to damage the rock.

But, there remain some impacts that must be considered and are most noticeable at more popular climbing locations such as Yosemite, Joshua Tree and the Shawangunks.

Chalk

Chalk is both a blessing and a curse. While it does help to improve a climber's grip by absorbing sweat and oils it is often overused. White smears are left plastered all over the rock. Frequently, holds become so thick with chalk that they turn slippery and must be cleaned off with a tooth brush before use. Perhaps the worst side-effect is that the calcium carbonate in chalk eats away at the rock leading to holds breaking off and general deterioration of the rock face.

Reduce your chalk use whenever possible. Climb when it is cooler. Chalk up less frequently. Use dirt as an alternative drying agent for your hands.

Tape

Many climbers will tape up their hands to prevent cuts and torn tissue. If you use tape, put it on and pack it out. Never tear off tape during a climb, even if soaked with sweat, and throw it down. Little pieces of tape lying all around the base and various routes of a climb are ugly.

Vegetation

The most noticeable impacts to vegetation occur near the base of many climbs. Climbers, anxious to begin the day quickly, choose any available route to get to the start, often creating a confusing network of paths. Many of these paths occur on steep, loose terrain and lead to major erosion problems. If a path exists, stick to it. If numerous paths are created, work with the park rangers or a local climbing club to block off and eliminate all but the best route to the climb.

Breaking off branches and sticks that are in the way during a climb may seem innocent enough, but this practice is not defensible. Work carefully around the vegetation or choose another route. It is never acceptable to alter the natural process or balance merely because something is in the way of your climb.

Modifying the rock

Sometimes, holds and placements in a rock are chiseled and hammered by a climber in an attempt to improve the hold or position of protection. This only serves to permanently damage the rock face and the climbing experience for others. Leave the rock as you found it. If you can't climb it clean, it wasn't meant to be climbed by you!

Figure 10-1 The over-anxious climber should stick to the path.

APPENDIX

Without A Trace "The Wilderness Challenge"
I Will:
–Plan ahead to avoid impact
–Avoid crowded dates and places
–Travel and camp in small groups
–Repackage food to reduce containers and trash
–Carry a litterbag to pack out all refuse
–Carry a stove and use foods requiring little cooking
–Use only gear with subdued colors
–Check with the Ranger Station for low-use areas
–Travel to avoid impacts
–Walk single file in the center of the trail
–Stay on the main trail even if wet or snow covered
–Never short-cut switchbacks
–Travel cross-country on rocky or timbered areas
–Look at and photograph, never pick or collect
–Stay at popular areas only briefly
–Make no-trace campsites
–Choose rocky, ridgetop, sandy and well-drained campsites
–Never cut trees or live wood
–Never dig holes, trenches or otherwise alter the campsite for convenience
–Build only small, safe campfires
–Use established fire rings when available
–Carry small firewood from well-stocked timbered areas outside the camp
–Set up camp two hundred feet away from the nearest water source or trail
–Wear soft-soled shoes around camp and avoid trampling vegetation
–Wash two hundred feet away from the nearest water source

–Urinate or defecate two hundred feet away from the nearest water source
–Use biodegradable soap only in small amounts and when necessary
–Prevent animal or human contact with human waste
–Pack out all litter and food scraps
–Animal-proof my camp and food
–Travel as quietly as possible
–Leave radios and tape players at home
–Pick up all litter, even other peoples
–Leave a no-trace campsite
–Erase all signs of a fire when appropriate
–Constantly look for signs of my passing and erase them if possible
–Apply the no-trace ethic everywhere, everyday

*excerpted and adapted with permission from, **Without a Trace,"The Wilderness Challenge...my personal answer to the wilderness challenge"**, by the U.S. Forest Service, Regional Office, San Francisco.

BIBLIOGRAPHY

For obtaining additional information regarding minimum impact camping techniques and environmental ethics I would suggest the following sources:

Backpacker Magazine, Rodale Press, 33 E. Minor St., Emmaus, PA
    18098 (215) 967-5171.
Buzzworm, The Environmental Journal, 1818 16th Street, Boulder,
    CO 80302 (303) 442-1969.
Canoe Magazine, P.O. Box 3146, Kirkland, WA 98083
    (206) 827-6363.
Outside Magazine, 1165 N. Clark St., Chicago, IL 60610
    (312) 951-0990.
Sierra Magazine, 730 Polk St., San Francisco, CA 94109
    (415) 776-2211.
Soft Paths, by Bruce Hampton and David Cole: Stackpole Books, 1988.
Walking Softly in the Wilderness, by John Hart: Sierra Club Books,
    1984
How to Shit in the Woods, by Kathleen Meyer: Ten Speed Press, 1989.
The Wilderness Educator, by the Wilderness Education Association:
    ICS Books, Inc., 1991.

INDEX